Living Reconciliation

A Preparation for Celebrating Forgiveness

Françoise Darcy-Berube and John Paul Berube

Child and Parent Book

MARINOUIC DANIEL+ROBERT

NOVALIS

ST. ANTHONY MESSENGER PRESS

Cincinnati, Ohio

CASSELL

Contents

Living Reconciliation builds on the main catechetical themes taught in Grades One and Two. It can be used as a complement to any curriculum. The program will bring welcome freshness, novelty, and liveliness to both children and teachers on their sacramental journey.

Living Reconciliation brings parents into direct conversation experience and celebration with their children. In clear, concrete ways it helps parents become the primary educators of their children, all the while fostering closer ties between the life of faith at home, in the classroom, and in the parish.

This work has been made possible through the collaboration of many people: parents, pastors, and catechists.

Created and written by:
Françoise Darcy-Bérubé and John-Paul Bérubé

Designed and illustrated by:
Benoit Jacques.

Acknowledgements:
Quotations from the Holy Scripture are adapted from *The Good News Bible.* Copyright © American Bible Society 1966, 1971, 1978.

Excerpts from the English translation of the *Rite of Penance* © 1974, International Committee on English in the Liturgy, Inc. All rights reserved.

The contents and approach of the *Living the Eucharist* program are in accord with *Sharing the Light of Faith, National Catechetical Directory for Catholics of the United States* issued by the United States Catholic Conference.

We are grateful for the collaboration of the National Office of Religious Education and the Canadian Conference of Catholic Bishops.

Imprimatur:
Rev. Bernard Hubert , Bishop of St. John-Longueuil, August 15, 1989.

Copyright ©1992: Novalis
6255 Hutchison, Outremont, Quebec, Canada H2V 4C7

Legal Deposit:
National Library, Ottawa, Canada.
National Library, Montreal, Canada

Distribution:
Novalis, 49 Front Street East, 2nd Floor
Toronto, Ontario, Canada M5E1B3

Distributed in United States by:
St. Anthony Messenger Press
1615 Republic St., Cincinnati, OH
45210-1298

Distributed in Great Britain and Ireland by:
Geoffrey Chapman, an imprint of Cassell
Wellington House, 125 Strand, London WC2R OBB

ISBN 2-89088-568-2

Printed in Canada

NOVALIS

1 Jesus Shows Us the Way

Here are some children your age.
You don't know their names,
but they are a lot like you.
They share with you a great dream:
they want to be happy!

Like you, these children are friends
of Jesus. They trust him and
want to follow him.
They know that with Jesus as their guide,
their dream will come true.
They will find the way to happiness!

In this group of children, you can see
an empty place. It is for you! Paste
or draw a picture of yourself there.

Let Us Listen to Jesus

When Jesus begins preaching, many people come to hear him. They like to listen to him because he is talking about something important to them. He is telling them *how to be happy.*

But he says some very surprising things. He does not say: "If you want to be happy, try to be the richest or the most beautiful or the strongest person in the world."

HAPPY ARE THOSE WHO LISTEN TO GOD'S WORD. HAPPY ARE THOSE WHO CARE. HAPPY ARE THOSE WHO MAKE PEACE.

No, instead Jesus says, "If you want to be truly happy, you must first seek the Kingdom of God... and keep the Law that was given to you:

Love the Lord your God with all your heart and love one another, because all of you are God's own children."

Yes, for Jesus the secret of happiness is the Law of Love.
This Law is a precious gift to us. It is a light on our path.

LOVE THE LORD YOUR GOD WITH ALL YOUR HEART

LOVE OTHERS AS YOU LOVE YOURSELF

Use some happy colors to draw
a frame around the Law of Love.

Jesus does more than just talk about the Law of Love;
he teaches us how to live by it every day. That is why,
in the following pages, we will look at Jesus.

Let Us Look at Jesus

Jesus teaches us how to follow the Law of Love; he is our guide, he will help us be happy.

Jesus spends the whole day in the town of Capernaum. He works hard and looks forward to resting. But towards evening the crowds bring many sick people to him.

When he sees how those people are suffering, Jesus feels sorrow for them, and he forgets how tired he is. He speaks kindly to each one of the sick people and lays his hands on them. He heals all of them.

Questions to think about:

- Why doesn't Jesus tell the people, "Come back tomorrow, I've worked all day, I'm tired"?

- How does Jesus greet the sick people? What does he do for them?

- After healing the sick, how does Jesus feel? Why does he feel this way?

- What does Jesus teach us in this story? Write your answer by completing the following sentence:

  We are happy when we H _____ P others.

One day, Jesus attends a wedding feast. The guests are having a wonderful time. They are singing, eating, talking, and dancing.

Suddenly something seems to worry the servants. They are running out of wine! Mary, Jesus' mother, sees what is happening...

What will Jesus do? Will he let the host be embarrassed because the guests have no more wine to drink? No!

Jesus sees six big empty jars. He tells the servants to fill them to the top with water...

The servants are amazed! Now the water is wine, and the wine is delicious! So the party continues, and everyone is happy.

Questions to think about:

- For whom did Jesus do the favor of changing the water into wine?

- Why do you think he did it?

- How did Jesus feel when he saw that the party would continue happily?

- What does Jesus teach us in this story?

  Jesus teaches us that we are happy when we_ _ _ _ and give_ _ _to others.

  Find the answer in the flowers.

7

Matthew is a tax collector; many people hate and despise him. Some people won't even talk to him.

One day, Jesus passes by Matthew's office. Instead of turning away from Matthew, Jesus stops, looks at him, and speaks to him with great *kindness.*

Matthew is surprised and so happy! Not only does Jesus talk to him, but Jesus invites him to become a friend, a disciple!

Matthew immediately leaves everything and follows Jesus.

One day, in the crowd that is following Jesus, a woman cries out very loudly. The woman is a stranger from a foreign country. She is making such a noise that the disciples ask Jesus to send her away.

Jesus is busy, talking to the people around him. Will he take time to listen to this stranger? Of course he will, because for Jesus each person is important and should be treated with *respect.*

Moved by the woman's trust, Jesus says to her: "You are a woman of great faith. What you want will happen." And he heals her daughter.

Questions to think about:

- **How do people treat Matthew and the foreign woman? Why?**
- **How does Jesus treat them? Why does Jesus act that way?**
- **How do you think Matthew and the foreign woman fell after meeting Jesus? Why?**
- **What does Jesus teach us in these stories?**

Jesus teaches us to treat everybody with _ _ _ _ _ _ _ _ and with _ _ _ _ _ _ _.
Find the two words in the stories.

1. Another of Jesus' friends is Peter. He is a fisherman who works very hard. One day, on the shore of the Sea of Galilee, Jesus asks Peter to follow him. Peter leaves his boat and his net and follows Jesus. They become very good friends.

Some years later, Jesus is arrested by his enemies and brought to court.

2. Peter stands outside the courtroom. He doesn't want anyone to recognize him. But a woman does recognize him. Peter is so afraid that he tells a lie.

Moments later, Peter understands that he has done a terrible thing. He has denied his friend Jesus. Peter is very, very sorry for what he has done.

3. A few days after the Resurrection, Jesus is with Peter again. Does he blame Peter for his being a coward? No, because Jesus has already forgiven Peter. Jesus only asks if he can still rely on Peter's love. Then Jesus makes Peter the leader of his Church. Jesus has never stopped trusting his friend Peter.

- If one of your friends did to you what Peter did to Jesus, how would you feel?
- Does Jesus have a good reason to say to Peter, "Just go away, you are not my friend anymore"?
  Why doesn't Jesus say this to Peter?
- What does Jesus teach us in this story?

Jesus teaches us that we should EGFORXAGIVEUMPR one another.

To find the word, strike out the extra letters.

Let Us Look at Jesus Again

One evening, Jesus stays with some of his friends.

The next morning, before sunrise, Jesus leaves the house.

When his friends get up, they discover that Jesus has left. They go out looking for him.

Finally, they find Jesus alone on a hillside. He is praying to God, his Father.

Jesus has many things to do, but he always finds time to pray, to listen to the Spirit. For Jesus, this is very important.

Jesus loves God his Father so much that he often speaks to him. When he walks in the countryside, Jesus admires all the wonders around him: the lake, the flowers, the sun, the birds. He praises God and thanks him for all the beauty in the world.

Jesus prays when he is happy; he shares his joy with God. He prays when he feels sad or afraid; he asks God for help.

As the Jewish people do, Jesus goes to God's house to pray with his friends.

He knows that to be truly happy we need to love and to trust God.

Draw Jesus praying with his friends.

Complete the following sentence:

Like Jesus we find joy and courage

when we L __ __ E God and P __ __ Y to God.

Completing the first step in your preparation

To follow Jesus
more closely:

- You might perhaps get to know Jesus better
  - by listening very carefully during your religion class,
  - by reading stories about Jesus with your parents.

- You might try to understand the Law of Love better
  - by reading the stories in this book very carefully,
  - by asking your parents to help you think about these stories.

Write or draw here what you have decided to do:

To review and remember:

This is what you learned:
- God gives us the Law of Love as a light on our path:

  Love the Lord your God
  with all your heart.
  Love others as you love yourself.

- Jesus is our guide, he wants us to be happy. Jesus shows us how to live, how to follow the Law of Love.

To help you pray:

Jesus,
I know you love me
and want me to be happy.
You teach me how to care
and forgive those who hurt me.
I thank you and I trust you.
Amen.

2 The Spirit of Jesus Is with Us

Peter and Matthew saw Jesus with their own eyes, they heard his voice, they walked along the lake with him. How wonderful it would be if we could do that also! But it is not possible because the Risen Lord has left this earth to return to God his Father.

However, we are very fortunate because we can be as close to Jesus as his friends Peter, Matthew, and the others. How can this happen?
It is thanks to the Holy Spirit who lives in our heart.

The Holy Spirit helps us to believe in Jesus, to know him and love him.
The Holy Spirit helps us live by the Law of Love, just as Jesus did.

Let us see what happens when we listen to the Spirit of Jesus.

Maybe you have heard stories about Saint Francis of Assisi. He lived long ago in beautiful Italy.

Like all of us, Francis wanted to be happy. But he wasn't. Then, one day, he understood that only Jesus could help him find true happiness. So he left his fine home and his riches to follow Jesus more closely.

Francis was very poor now, but he had found a great treasure. The peace and joy of God were in his heart!

Francis wanted to know God better. So, he prayed for many hours. Sometimes he prayed at night under the stars.

Francis of Assisi wanted to share the joy he had found in loving God. So, he walked up and down the countryside, speaking to people about God's love.

Francis saw such beauty in the world that he often sang with joy. He praised God with all his heart. People said that, sometimes, even the birds gathered to listen to him and to sing with him!

When we listen to the Spirit of Jesus, we discover, like Francis did, the joy of loving God.

Because she loves God, Susan wants to pray every day.
Each morning she offers God her new day.

THANK YOU, GOD, FOR THIS NEW DAY. I OFFER IT TO YOU WITH JOY. HELP ME LIVE IT IN YOUR LOVE.

In the evening there is no rush, so Susan takes more time to pray.
Sometimes she reads a Gospel story and thinks about it.

No one ever loved God as much as the Virgin Mary did. That is why we often ask Mary to help us grow in love.

Write here a prayer to Mary.

Paste here a beautiful picture of Mary.

"There is more happiness in giving than in receiving." ACTS 20:35

Elizabeth Fry lived in England more than 150 years ago. She was rich and lived happily with her husband and her children in a beautiful house.

But then the Spirit of Jesus helped her discover the joy of caring for others, of building a better world.

She learned about a terrible prison for women where their children had to stay with them. (In those days nobody cared much about the people living in prison. Many of the prisoners, including children, died of hunger, cold or disease.)

Elizabeth understood that the Spirit of Jesus was asking her to do something to help these women. So, she visited them in prison every day and brought them help and comfort.

People began to call her the Angel of the prison. Following her example, Elizabeth's friends began to come to the prison with her to care for the prisoners.

Gradually the poor women in prison found new courage and new hope, and they began to help one another.

16

When we open our heart to the Spirit of Jesus, we discover, like Elizabeth did, the joy of caring for others.

The Holy Spirit does not ask all of us to do what Elizabeth did. No. The Spirit of Jesus invites us to find simple ways to help people around us be happy. Then we make the world a better place to live in.

Have you ever had a wonderful idea about how to care for others? Write or draw here what you did.

- Why did you do that?
- How did you help people be happy that day?
- How did you feel afterwards? Why did you feel that way?
- How do you think God felt? Why?

Let's Share Our Good Ideas

Read each of the stories on these two pages. Think about them. Then imagine how they could end if the children in the stories listened to the Spirit of Jesus.

Mother hasn't seen Patrick but Pat knows that his mother is very tired. She has worked hard all day getting the twins ready for camp.

Draw in the picture what Patrick might do.

Stephanie is very upset. Once again she's been given a low mark in math. She thinks she will never become a third grader.

What could Stephanie's friends do to help her? Write or draw it here.

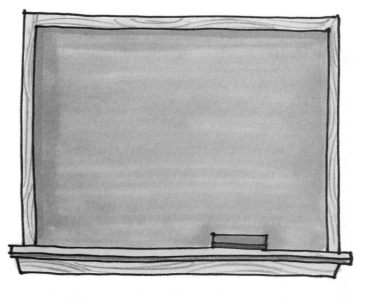

Many times Daddy has scolded Carole for leaving her toys lying in front of the garage door. When he comes home from work, he has to get out of the car and move the toys. This makes him angry.

One afternoon, Carole is playing outside the garage. A friend passes by and invites her to come and play.

What will Carole do?

COME, CAROLE, WE ARE GOING TO PLAY AT JOSE'S...

Nancy and Thomas have just moved into a new neighborhood. They've already made many friends.

But they often notice an old lady, sitting alone near a window; she seems very sad.

LOOK, NANCY, IT'S MRS. JOLY COMING BACK FROM THE STORE.

YES, HER BAGS ARE TOO HEAVY FOR HER.

Nancy and Thomas would like to help Mrs. Joly. They talk to their parents about it. What good ideas could they find together to make Mrs. Joly happier?

A Thousand Ways to Love

When we listen to the Spirit of Jesus, we discover many wonderful ways of showing our love for God and for other people.

When we live by the Law of Love, God's light is in our heart and we build a better world, a world like God wants it to be.

Write the matching word or words near each picture:

help - encourage - be grateful - comfort - obey - care - share - pray - forgive - make peace - give thanks -

"I love your Law,
it is a light on my path.
I love your Law,
it is the joy of my heart!"
Psalms 118

The rainbow has many different colors, and they are all beautiful.

Each family, each class is gifted with many different talents, and they are all important.

God wants us to develop our talents so we can grow and be happy.

God wants us to share our talents so we can make other people happy, too.

Ask some members of your family or of your class to write here the talent you have that they enjoy the most.

_____

_____

_____

_____

Now write here the talent you enjoy the most in some of these people.

_____

_____

_____

Prayer

**O Loving God,
we thank you for our talents
and for the joy they give us.
Help us to use our talents
to make other people happy, too.
Amen.**

Completing the second step in your preparation

To follow Jesus
more closely:

- You might pray to God more often.
- You might work hard to develop your talents.
- You might think of ways to make people happier around you:
  at home,
  in school,
  in your neighborhood.

Write or draw here what you
have decided to do:

To review and remember:

This is what you learned:

- The Spirit of Jesus is with us
  to help us know and love God,
  to help us pray as Jesus did.
- The Spirit of Jesus is with us
  to help us care for one another,
  to help us forgive one another,
  as Jesus did.
- When we listen in our heart
  to the Spirit of Jesus,
  we find the joy and peace of God.

To help you pray:

Come, Spirit of light,
teach us how to pray
and to listen to God's call.

Come, Spirit of love,
give us the strength we need
to make a better world.

Come, Spirit of peace,
help us trust the Lord
and fill our heart with joy.
Amen. Alleluia!

3 God Always Forgives Us

When we listen to the Spirit of Jesus, we build a friendly world: we care, we share and forgive one another. Everyone is happier in a friendly world.

But we do not always listen to the Holy Spirit. Too often, we close our heart, and forget about the Law of Love. We become selfish and unfair, and we hurt one another. The world we build around us is not friendly any more.

What does God think of all that? Of course, God does not like us to hurt each other. God does not want us to make people unhappy.

But, as Jesus shows us in the Gospel, God's love is so great that he never turns away from us. God is always ready to forgive us, to help us change and do better, so we can be happy again.

What Happens When We Don't Want to Listen to the Spirit of Jesus?

Questions to think about:

- How does Pedro feel about losing his car?

- What do you think of what Xavier did?

- What does Jesus think about what Xavier did?

- How do you think Xavier feels after hearing what his father said?

Living Reconciliation

A Preparation for Celebrating Forgiveness

Françoise Darcy-Berube and John Paul Berube

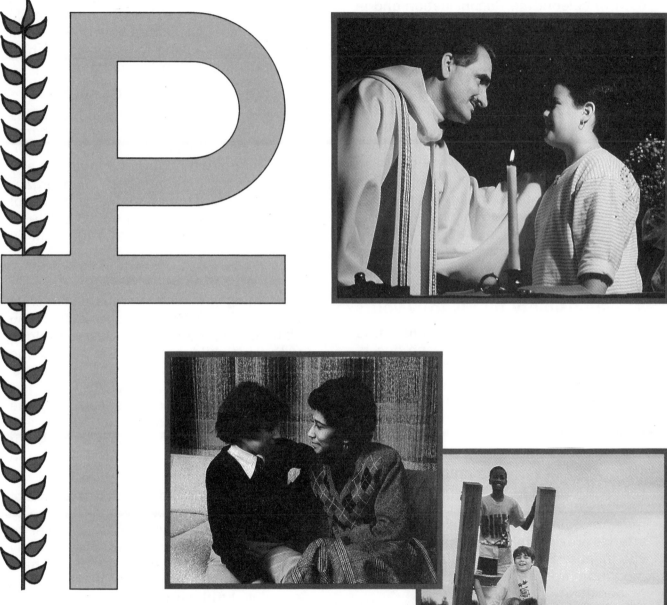

Parent Guide

CLAUDE PRIMEAU
& ASSOCIATES
Scarborough,
Ontario, Canada

GEOFFREY
CHAPMAN
London
U.K.

FRANCISCAN
COMMUNICATIONS
Los Angeles,
California, U.S.A.

Introduction

An invitation from your Christian community

As children reach the age of reason, the Church happily extends to them a special invitation to join their parish community both in celebrating Reconciliation and in sharing the Bread of Life. All children, says the Church, should be prepared for the sacraments and offered the possibility of celebrating them. However, the family decides whether to celebrate them or not. The Church invites parents to make that decision with their child after considering whether she or he wishes to and is ready to fully celebrate those sacraments.

The book you have in hand is designed to help you prepare your child at home in a relaxed and happy atmosphere for the Sacrament of Reconciliation. Another beautiful book called *Living the Eucharist* is also available to help you do the same for your child's First Communion.

A responsibility that is truly yours

No one can adequately replace you in this joy-filled task simply because no one is closer to your child than yourselves. Better than anyone else, you can give your child the opportunity to experience God's loving mercy, through your own forgiving and healing love.

That is why the Church entrusts to you the task of preparing your child for the Sacrament of Reconciliation. The ongoing religious education classes that your child attends provide the basic instruction he or she needs. But your child's immediate preparation is truly your privilege and responsibility.

A task you began long ago

You've been preparing your child for a long time! Indeed, just remember how often, over the past years, you have patiently taught your child to say "I'm sorry" or "It's O.K., I forgive you" or "Let's be friends again!"

While helping resolve the normal daily conflicts of family life, while lovingly forgiving your child, over and over again, you have no doubt prepared that child to open her or his heart to God's tender mercy. Now you can go one step further in the same direction: you can help your child become more explicitly aware of God's call and of God's loving forgiveness, both in our daily life and in the sacrament.

A community ready to help

However, you are not alone in facing this task. Your Christian community shares your responsibility and is eager to help you. That is why you need to attend any parents' meeting your parish might organize. Likewise, if your parish or your school offers special classes for the children, these would certainly enrich your child's preparation.

A simple and easy means

Everything you need to prepare your child is in the Child's Book. No special teaching skills are required to use it. Just read along with your child, enjoying the stories and the pictures, discussing the questions, and doing the activities. Feel free to use only what you think your child is ready for at the present time. The book is rich and varied, and your child will enjoy coming back to it with you for many months after the celebration.

Preparing your child for the Sacrament of Reconciliation can be a wonderful opportunity for both of you to grow closer to each other and also to God. We sincerely hope that *Living Reconciliation* can help you make that preparation both meaningful and delightful, so your whole family can celebrate with joy the feast of God's loving mercy. "Come, rejoice with me, for I have found my lost sheep," says the Lord.

Guidelines

When to begin

The *Living Reconciliation* program is made up of four themes, which you may cover in three to four weeks at your convenience. If your parish or school offers special classes for the children, these will greatly enrich what you do at home. However, don't worry if for any reason your child cannot take part in these. Carefully going through the book at home with your child is a sufficient preparation.

What you will find in your Guide

For each theme you will find four sections:

● the first one— *Growing in faith as Christian adults* —helps you enrich and deepen your own Christian life and your understanding of the theme;

● the second one— *Understanding our children and helping them grow* — presents practical suggestions for the moral education of your child;

● the third one— *Experiencing the theme at home* —offers simple guidelines for using the Child's Book;

● the fourth one provides you with *Suggestions for daily life and prayer.*

How to get started

A few days before you intend to begin, leaf through the Child's Book to get the feel of it. Then read in your book the first two sections related to Theme One. Take time to enjoy these sections and to think about them.

Before beginning Theme One with your child, make sure you have read all the child's pages on this theme as well as the corresponding suggestions in your Parents' Guide: *Experiencing the theme at home.*

What to do along with your child

You will need only to read together the pages specified for each conversation, to comment on the pictures, and to discuss with the child the proposed questions.

Each of the conversations may last about fifteen minutes, sometimes more, sometimes less, according to the subject and your child's experience and understanding. Each theme suggests some project that your child can carry out on his or her own, such as drawing, coloring, making a poster.

Learning is more fruitful when the activity time immediately follows the conversation. When this is not possible, you must recreate the atmosphere of the conversation before inviting your child to complete the activity. When your child has finished, ask him or her to comment on the activity and add your own remarks to reinforce the message.

The suitable atmosphere

A good preparation can be carried out only in an atmosphere of joy, love, and prayer. Your child needs to experience these weeks of preparation not as an obligation but rather as a joyful occasion to prepare to meet the Lord Jesus in a special way.

The best way to achieve this climate is to set aside, with your child, a special time for these conversations. Avoid conflict with his or her favorite occupations: skating, swimming, a special TV program. Furthermore, do not hurry your child. Put off a session until the next day rather than rush through it.

Importance of evening prayer

The preparation for First Reconciliation is an ideal time to help your child make daily prayer a lifetime habit. If you don't already pray daily together, set aside a few minutes every evening, or whenever possible, for praying with your child (not "making him or her pray"). For each theme you will find a variety of simple suggestions for making these moments a rich and happy experience for both you and your child.

Theme One: Jesus Shows Us the Way

Growing in faith as adults

The one thing we all seek is happiness! Advertisers know this well. They constantly try to seduce us, offering ''no risk'' recipes for happiness through beauty, comfort, success, prestige, travel.

Jesus also invites us to happiness. But Jesus offers us much more than mere superficial happiness, he proposes to us an incredible challenge: to seek our happiness in the manner of God!

''God is love,'' writes John the Evangelist, and God's delight is to love, to create life, communion, joy. But how can we ever love in the manner of God? To meet that challenge would we not need to see with our own eyes and hear with our own ears what God would be and do as a human being? Yes, indeed. And behold, the Word became flesh and walked our human paths. Jesus shared our risks and struggles, our joys and suffering, our deep longing for happiness. That is not all. To awaken in our human heart the taste for divine happiness and the courage to seek it, God gives us his Spirit.

Christian morality then consists in seeking our happiness by walking in the footsteps of Jesus. When we respond to God's call, to God's invitation, we accept the risk and the challenge of following Jesus.

Maybe you think this is fine for adults but can have no meaning for children. Aren't they much too young to understand any of this? Let the children answer. Among many others, here is the true story of Mary Lou!

Today Grade 2 is celebrating with games and a party. The principal visits the class and gives each child a roll of candy. Everyone is enjoying the candy except Mary Lou.

-Mary Lou, why aren't you eating your candies? Look at your friends. They're all enjoying them.
-Sure, they are laughing with their mouths now! But tonight at home, when I share mine with my family, I will laugh in my heart!

What do we learn from Mary Lou and so many children who often surprise us? We learn two important things:

Children are indeed capable of appreciating the kind of ''God-like happiness'' we were talking about. Mary Lou is like any other child who enjoys the healthy pleasures of playing, eating candy, winning at sports, or playing tricks. But she is also able to appreciate a different quality of joy, the joy of sharing a treat, of giving pleasure to others at her own expense.

The moral sensitivity and behavior of children are often in advance of their ability to verbalize and explain their moral intuitions. Mary Lou may not be able to explain anything about different qualities of

joy. But in her own naive and charming way, she has said it all! Someone wrote one day, commenting on the morality Jesus proposes: ''We must choose the way that offers the best quality of joy.'' This indeed can be our guiding light for moral education.

Understanding our children and helping them grow

Up to seven or eight years of age, the moral life of children is dominated by what is allowed and what is forbidden. What is wrong is what displeases adults and brings punishment. What is right is what pleases them and brings reward. This is a pre-moral stage.

But around the age of reason the child's moral judgment gradually becomes more enlightened, more personal. This usually happens in flashes: one area of the child's life is touched by a new moral insight, then another, and so on over a number of years. In the process of developing his or her social life in the family, in school, or in the neighborhood, the child will discover new values, like Mary Lou experienced different qualities of joy.

This is when Jesus' call and his Law of Love can very naturally be explained. Jesus might be introduced as the friend who wants to help us experience more and more that precious kind of joy that makes us ''laugh in our heart.'' And the children will discover the Law of Love as a guiding light on their path.

To encourage moral growth in our children at that stage, we should avoid deciding and judging everything for them. Instead we should help them explore their own insights and listen to the Lord's call. This will ultimately enable them to decide what to do and how to judge their actions.

Experiencing the theme at home

• Goals

-To understand that Jesus is our guide on the way to true happiness.

- To want to follow Jesus with trust.

If the children attend a Group Session, they will talk about sacraments as special signs of Jesus' love. They will be given a poster of Jesus evoking Baptism and the two other sacraments they are invited to celebrate this year.

• Preparations

Contact your parish or school to get precise information about any Group Sessions or special activities for your child.

• Conversations with your child

Note: The following suggestions are divided in three brief sections, each dealing with a few pages of the Child's Book. Feel free, however, to follow your own pace.

1. Tell your child about the possibility that he or she might join the parish community in celebrating the Sacrament of Reconciliation.

Give your child the Child's Book and explain that together you will use it during special times set aside just for sharing. Decide with your child the days, times, and place most suitable so you can fully enjoy these moments together.

Admire together and comment on the front cover. Ask the child the meaning of the yellow symbol and the olive branch; explain it if necessary. Point out the following : *Mother and child are making peace after a big argument. How do they feel now? A priest is kindly giving a child the sign of God's forgiveness. The two scenes remind us that celebrating the Sacrament helps us live reconciliation in our daily life. And what does the bottom picture say? It is fun to be friends!*

Read page 3 and invite your child to paste or draw his or her picture in the empty space.

Read pages 4 and 5, and have your child do the activity. Speak about your own trust in Jesus, explaining the prayer on page 12. Then say the prayer together and encourage your child to learn it by heart.

2. Read pages 6 to 12, and comment on the gospel stories at leisure. Depending on your child's personality and the setting in which you live, talk about the stories of Matthew and of the foreign woman if there is some tension in your child's school or the neighborhood because of differences in race, religion or language. However, if your child tends to hold a grudge, discuss more fully the story of Peter. Occasionally tell your child how the Law of Love helps you make the right choices.

3. Together look again at page 3, the title page. Read also the brief review on page 12. Help your child make a realistic choice about what he or she wants to do to follow Jesus. Encourage your child to memorize the Law of Love.

Suggestions for daily life and prayer

● Often say together the prayer on page 12.

● When your child asks a question related to simple moral choices that he or she has to make, do not provide an answer. To encourage your child to think for himself or herself, ask such questions as: *"What do you think you should do? Why? What do you think Jesus would have done?"*

● Occasionally comment on the loving choices your child makes, showing how they make him or her more like Jesus.

● Discuss the religion classes your child attends. Encourage your child to participate in them actively so he or she can know Jesus better and follow him more closely.

Theme two: The Spirit of Jesus Is with Us

Growing in faith as adults

"I will send you my Spirit to be with you forever," said Jesus. Only the Spirit of God can enable us, restless and earthly mortals, to find true happiness in sharing ourselves and giving our life even to the point of death as Jesus did. This is so because all true love comes from God: "God has poured out his love into our hearts by means of the Holy Spirit who is God's gift to us" (Rom 5:5).

God's love is creative energy capable of accomplishing in our heart "much more than we can ever ask for or even think of" (Eph 3:20). Inasmuch as we open our heart to the Spirit, we will be increasingly transformed into the "image and likeness of Christ." The Spirit will lead us gently to share in Christ's own attitudes (2 Cor 3:18 and Phil 2:5). In our effort to love as Jesus did, we must constantly "leave death and come over into life" (1 Jn 3:14). While the effort is ours, it is inspired and energized by the Spirit. This work of salvation gradually frees us from the fears and selfishness of our "old self." This gift of God leads us to the joy of new life, to "the freedom of God's children," for "where the Spirit of the Lord is present, there is freedom" (2 Cor 3:18).

That new life will transform and shape our relationships and our way of life: "You are called to be free. But do not let that freedom become an excuse for evil... Instead let love make you serve one another" (based on Gal 5:13). And the fruit of life in the Spirit will be love, joy, peace, patience, kindness, goodness, faithfulness, humility and self-control" (Gal 5:22).

As we rediscover these amazing realities of our faith, we understand why Augustine could sum up the whole Christian morality in one phrase: "Love, and do whatever you want. "It is another way of saying what Paul had written to the Galatians: "If the Spirit has given us life, he must also control our lives" (Gal 5:25).

Christian morality is creative and imaginative. In saying "Thou shalt not kill," the Law imposes a negative limit, while emphasizing a positive command: "Thou shalt respect life." Our task with the help of the Spirit, is to use our moral imagination to discover, generation after generation, the concrete demands of this commandment. For too many people, unfortunately, Christian morality seems reduced to "not doing anything wrong." The real thrust of Christian morality, however, is described by Jesus when he says "Love one another as I have loved you" (Jn 13:34).

Understanding our children and helping them grow

There are two aspects to a child's moral education: the development of moral judgment, which occurs mainly through dialogue about daily experience; and the formation of a child's drive and will. The real challenge in moral education lies not in teaching the children the commandments and the fear of doing wrong. The real challenge is to motivate them to freely choose to do good. In other words, to awaken in them the taste for good, like one awakens a taste for beauty, for music. This "taste" gives children the desire and the will to effectively do good. Here a few suggestions to do just that:

• Give your child the opportunity to experience different qualities of joy, in particular the joy of caring, sharing, encouraging. This kind of joy is "like sunshine in my heart" as a seven-year-old child once said. Occasionally, share with your child your own experience of that joy, as the child does with you. In doing that you reinforce the meaning and impact of those experiences.

• Bring your child to the awareness of the presence of the Holy Spirit in our heart. Stress that the Spirit helps us discern the Law of Love and gives us peace and joy when we live by this Law. Frequently children live in the company of an "invisible friend." They often do so without our being aware of it. Let us take advantage of the imaginative ability of our children for the development of their spiritual life.

6

We have witnessed many times the joyful complicity that can exist between a child and the Holy Spirit. Coming home from school, a child named Teddy showed his mother a drawing on which we see different persons alone in their rooms.

After explaining who the persons were in each room, Teddy asked with a twinkle in his eye: *"Mother, do you think each person is alone in the room?"* *"It seems to me they are,"* said the mother unaware of the trap. *"Well they are not,"* said Teddy triumphantly, *"because the Spirit of Jesus is with each one of them!"* Asked what the Spirit was doing, Teddy answered: *"The Spirit is giving them good ideas to do nice things."* It is to stimulate the moral imagination of the child that many different examples are used in this theme.

• Another means of fostering your child's moral creativity and imagination is to personalize the Law of Love. Depending on our personal talents or qualities and on the circumstances of our lives, God's call will touch us in different ways and our response will be different.

Nancy was rightly happy and proud to be the best speller in her class. She never missed an occasion to point out that her best friend, Susan, made a lot of mistakes. But one day, her mother tactfully helped her discover a special responsibility linked to her talent. A simple question was enough: *"I understand how happy you are that you had no mistakes in your spelling,"* she said. *"But don't you think Susan would be happy, too, if someone helped her do better?"* The spontaneous reaction was typical of a child's egocentricism: *"Well... sure she would... but I like being better than she is!"* The matter was closed. But the question found its way into the heart of the child. A few days later, a happy and excited Nancy came home and rushed to her mother: *"You know, Mother, we were to have spelling this afternoon and Susan was scared. So after lunch at recess, I helped her prepare and she only made three mistakes. The teacher congratulated her, and she was so happy!"* Nancy's mother and the Invisible Friend in her heart had helped the child discover a new responsibility in using her talents and a different quality of joy!

Experiencing the theme at home

• Goals

- To understand that the Spirit of Jesus is with us to help us find in our own heart good ideas to live the Law of Love.

- To appreciate more consciously and more deeply the special joy we experience when we love and care.

• Preparations
(supplementary activities)

A child's booklet on a saint (activity 1).
A box and index cards (activity 2).
For activity 3, see the celebration.

If the children attend a Group Session, they will share their good ideas on how to make a better world in their school, their neighborhood, and with their friends in sport's clubs, on playgrounds.

• Conversations with your child

1. Read and comment on page 13, the title page. Ask questions like the following:

"Who is there? What are they doing? How do they feel?"

Read pages 14 and 15. Stress the joy we find in praying to the Lord like Francis did: *"Isn't it a privilege to be able to talk to God any time we want! Who else is always ready to listen to us?"* Stress how prayer is an important means of showing our love for God. Have your child do the activity on page 15. Write out a prayer of your own on a card and give it to your child.

Read pages 16 and 17. Have your child do the drawing on page 17. Take time to share in depth the questions of page 17. Encourage your child to express and appreciate the feelings he or she experienced in carrying out the action in the drawing.

End the conversation by saying together the prayer to the Spirit on page 22. **See supplementary activity 1.**

2. Read and discuss pages 18 and 19. When your child has expressed her or his ideas, you might add yours. Stress the positive effects of the loving choices on all the people involved.

Conclude by reading page 20 and doing the activity. Point out that the Spirit of Jesus wants to help us use our imagination to find wonderful ideas for creating happiness around us. Share your good ideas. Discuss also some of the difficulties of family life. Stress that these difficulties are normal: *"We have to learn to share many things at home: the parents' attention and time, the TV, the space, the chores. The Lord does not ask us to be a perfect family. No, instead the Lord asks us to be a family that constantly tries to overcome our problems and to grow in love together.* **See supplementary activity 2.**

3. Read page 21. Tell your child the talents and good qualities you most appreciate in him or her. Write them in the book. Ask other family members to do this also. Have your child do the same for the other members of your family. Say together the prayer on page 21. Help your child become aware of the special responsibility to develop her or his talents.

Read page 22 and have your child write what he or she has decided to do. Make sure the choice is realistic.

Turn again to the title page, page 13. Then read the review on page 22. Check to see if your child truly understands the statements. Encourage him or her to learn them by heart. **See supplementary activity 3.**

Suggestions for daily life and prayer

• Whenever suitable, encourage your child to appreciate more consciously the joy we experience whenever we make loving choices even if sometimes they are very demanding. Increase his or her awareness of the happiness our loving choices create around us. Share those experiences together.

Stress that the Spirit gives us the gift to experience and appreciate the joy of caring. Give thanks for it.

• During evening prayer, encourage your child to think about the decision he or she has made on how to follow Jesus better.

• Occasionally say the prayers composed by the child and yourself on page 15 and also the prayers on pages 21 and 22.

Supplementary activities

1. Read the life of a saint to your child, stressing how the saint lived the Law of Love. Describe other examples closer to the life of your child.

2. Choose one of the following activities:
- Prepare a wish-box where each member of the family could put one or two cards with a good idea to make life in the family even happier.

-Play the "Happy Face Game." Invite each family member to try and make the people they meet smile by doing them a favor, saying a kind word. In the evening each family member is encouraged to share his or her stories. Then as a family thank God for helping you love and create happiness.

3.   A family celebration

The following plan is proposed only as an example. Use your family's ideas to make this project even better. The celebration may take place in the even-

ing before dinner or at bed time. If it takes place before dinner, the family table would be a good setting since this will also lay a foundation for your child to perceive more vividly, later on, the strong symbolism of the Eucharistic meal.

Preparations

-Prepare beforehand a colored card and a small candle for each person; scotch tape or pieces of string to attach the cards to the candles; a large candle to symbolize Jesus' light; a bouquet, which could be arranged around the large candle; perhaps a newly baked loaf of bread.

-Recall events of daily life: On the eve of the celebration, ask each member of your family to remember an occasion when he or she was happy because of another's kindness. Then invite each family member to write the incident on a colored card.

The celebration

The dinner table is set, the small unlit candles are on the table. When the celebration starts, dim the lights or close the drapes. Give the child preparing for the Sacrament of Reconciliation the large lit candle.to carry. Have each person bring the card he or she has filled in. Gather your family at the threshold of the dining room.

- **Introduction by a parent**

"We have come together this evening to celebrate the joy of living together as a family, to celebrate God's love inviting us to live in his light and his peace."

Invite your family to proceed to the table singing a song of joy and praise. Help the child carrying the large candle to put it down on the table. Then continue:

"When we care for one another, our hearts and our home are full of light, of love, of joy! Let us recall together moments when a gesture of love from someone brought us light and joy."

- **Celebrating the rite**

Starting with the parents (so as to show the children what to do) each one in turn performs the following rite:

• Mother reads her flash card: *"Because Linda prepared dinner for the little ones, Daddy and I were able to go out."*

• Mother lights a candle from the large candle, offers the newly lit candle to Linda, and says: *"Because you did that for me the other day, light and joy filled my heart!"*

- Mother then attaches her flash card to Linda's candle.

- Linda places her lighted candle at a predetermined spot, near the large candle or the bouquet.

- This gesture is repeated until each has placed his or her candle.

- Reading the Word of God

One of the family members then says: *"Let us listen to the Word of God. What we did will help us understand God's words to us."*

God is light. There is no darkness in God. When we love others, our heart is filled with light. We then are united with God because God is light. When we dislike others we walk in darkness, the light of God is not in us. Let us live as children of light. (Adapted from John 5; 1 John 2; Eph 5).

After the reading, spend a short time in silence.

- Sharing the Word of God (3 or 4 minutes)

Using a dialogue format emphasize the following ideas: *"This large candle represents God's light, God's love which was awakened in our heart by the Spirit of Jesus... God makes us able to love because God wants to share with us the joy of loving. For this joy given to us, let us thank and praise God together."*

- Praying together

God our loving Parent, you share with us the joy of loving, you give us your Spirit who helps us to love a little bit as you do. We offer you our joy and give you thanks for it. Amen.

Sing a song of praise and thanksgiving. If the celebration is held just before supper, immediately share the meal. If bread was baked, offer and share it in the spirit of the celebration.

Theme Three: God Always Forgives Us

Growing in faith as adults

• What is sin?

"Love, and do whatever you want," Saint Augustine told us. "Let the Spirit control your life," said Saint Paul. Apparently if we let ourselves be carried by the power of love, we will achieve spiritual freedom and holiness! Unfortunately, we encounter difficulty, for as Paul laments, "I don't do the good I want to do; instead, I do the evil that I do not want to do!" (Rom 7:19).

Who, among us, could not make that same complaint? Indeed, within our depths we are divided beings. We experience an inner struggle, a constant gap between what we are and what we wish to be. Within us dwells affinity with God, an impetus that opens us to the happiness God offers us. Yet we also suffer a sluggishness, a hardheartedness, a secret fear that causes us to avoid the risk of opening our heart to love.

Psychologists have noticed these contradictory forces within us. The Bible speaks of grace and sin, light and darkness, life and death, to describe these forces. In short, insofar as we are honest with ourselves, we have to acknowledge with Paul "that sin lives in us" (Rom 7:20).

Sin is a religious reality. We can only acknowledge our sinfulness inasmuch as God is real for us, inasmuch as the fundamental goal of our life is in the light of God's plan, of God's call. However, the presence of sin in our life is not always spectacular. Sin often creeps in like a corrosive spiritual anemia. It becomes the fruit of hundreds of minor choices, apparently harmless, that furtively lower us to a selfish and materialist mediocrity, to a norm of values that is the very opposite of the mandate of the gospels. Consequently we have great need of the help of the Spirit to become aware of our sinfulness.

• What does God do in the face of sin?

Jesus describes the "unreasonable" behavior of the prodigal son's father as a parable of God's own attitude towards his sinful children. God's mercy, God's offer of salvation is at the very heart of the revelation of the Kingdom. However, in spite of his infinite love and power, God cannot save us if we do not welcome his forgiveness, if we do not trust in the happiness he offers us. This accounts for the urgency of God's call to conversion running throughout the gospels.

What is really expressed is the anxious plea of a Father who cannot permit his children to bring about their own unhappiness. Doesn't the present state of the world give us an idea—on a planetary level—of the misery God wanted to save us from when he sent Jesus to us? And Jesus took so seriously his struggle to free us from our spiritual blindness and sin that he died for us.

Welcoming God's saving love, welcoming God's forgiveness is what conversion is about. As Christians, we know we can never be imprisoned by our past because God's forgiveness is a new creation. With God we can always start again: "Behold I make all things new," says the Lord (Rev 21:5).

The God of Jesus Christ, then, is not a Great Policeman nor a Big Daddy who watches us nor is he an Indulgent Father. The God of Jesus Christ is a God who takes our sinfulness very seriously because our dignity and our happiness is of grave importance. God forgives us even before we ask and is ready to do anything to save us, but God cannot reconcile us if we do not change direction. Jesus speaks of God as a father who throws a huge party, when his son who went astray comes home because he is hungry!

Understanding our children and helping them grow

The first awareness of sin is an important stage in the moral and spiritual development of your child. Indeed that awareness will decisively shape the child's image of God. The following suggestions might prove helpful in leading your child through that stage.

• Don't make God a factor in the pre-moral formation of your child. The apprenticeship of life together—good manners, family rules, basic respect for other people—must rest on your own loving and firm authority and not on God's authority. God is not a means at the service of our educational endeavour!

• Don't be in a hurry. Before even mentioning the reality of sin, you need to provide your child with two types of ongoing experiences: the experience of being loved and called by God to happiness; the experience of being forgiven and healed within the family.

• Help your child enrich and deepen his or her relationship with God through the experience of sin. Here are a few suggestions:

- Agree with your child's new awareness, stressing that you too share the experience: *"It is true, that when we act that way, when we choose to do wrong, we displease God, we are sinners."*

- Immediately arouse a feeling of trust: *"Even when we sin, God still loves us; God forgives us and wants to help us do better."* Arouse also a feeling of contrition: *"When we know how much God loves us, we are sorry for what we did, and we ask God to forgive us."* When forgiving your child, occasionally evoke God's loving presence also forgiving him or her.

• Avoid certain mistakes. Do not use any comments that could deform your child's image of God: *"God is angry at you... God will punish you... Jesus is crying."* Do not use any comments that could unfavorably affect your child's self-image. Your attitude should bring your child to think: *"I did something mean, but I can do better."* It should never lead your child to think: *"I am mean, and I can do nothing about it."*

• Use patient, loving dialogue to foster your child's moral maturation. Psychologists as well as educators agree on the importance of this. However, let us recall that, like ourselves, the child may not be ready at all times for real dialogue. A stern "lecture" on the spot doesn't bear much fruit. Dialogue requires attentive listening as well as speaking.

• Take advantage of everyday incidents to help your child become more consciously aware of his or her intentions. Lead your child to distinguish clearly between a mishap, a mistake, and a sin (an unloving choice).

Bring your child to reflect on his or her actions in the light of God's call. Avoid evaluating and judging them yourself for your child.

Experiencing the theme at home

• Goals

- To develop a practical understanding of the different aspects of conversion.

- To acquire a deep trust in God's loving forgiveness.

• Preparations

For the celebration: everything that was required or used in Theme 2.

If the children attend a Group Session, they will act out different scenarios to help them make a clear distinction between a sin, a mishap, a mistake, a temptation. They will hear a gospel story about Jesus' kindness to sinners.

• Conversations with your child

1. Read the title page, page 23, and comment on the picture: *"Who is there? What is happening? How do they feel? Why do we have the two pictures?"*

Read the stories on pages 24, 25 and 26. Help your child think about the different consequences of the people's actions. Bring up similar situations experienced by yourself and your child. Discuss them together.

Make sure your child understands clearly the difference between a mistake, a mishap, and a fault we do "on purpose."

Make sure your child understands the final text on page 26: God forbids certain things so as to protect us against evil and harm.

2. Read and discuss the story on pages 27 and 28. Have the child do the drawing. Discuss the questions.

Tell your child how you feel when you have the opportunity to forgive him or her. Recall an occasion when you had to be forgiven; explain how you felt then. Help your child understand that all of us have to forgive one another like this. Show how in doing so we learn to love one another even more.

Read page 29. Stress Jesus' kindness as a reflection of God's kindness. If your child knows other stories about Jesus forgiving sinners, let him or her tell about them.

Express your personal trust in Jesus. Encourage your child to learn a prayer of sorrow like the one on page 34.

Read with your child what is suggested on page 34 under the title "What could you do to follow Jesus more closely?" Explain the importance of the habits described there. Suggest that you might do the examination of conscience together every evening

until the celebration, to help your child develop the habit of doing it on his or her own.

3. Read pages 30 and 31. Share ideas to help your child understand that we have many different ways to say we are sorry. Using the questions on page 31 encourage your child's self expression and share your own experiences.

Read page 32 and discuss the questions. After your child has expressed his or her own ideas, express yours.

Read page 33. Encourage your child to genuinely express his or her difficulties in forgiving others and accepting reconciliation. Express your own difficulties. Then stress the relief and joy we experience when we have finally forgiven someone and are together again!

Take the time to read with your child the review statements on page 34. Make sure your child understands them. **See supplementary activity.**

Suggestions for daily life and prayer

• Take advantage of negative incidents to gently help your child become aware of the different steps involved in the conversion process: we acknowledge our responsibility: "It is my fault..."; we tell God we are sorry, and we also tell others; we show we are sorry by making up for the wrong we did, by accepting reconciliation.

• Take time to experience fully forgiveness and reconciliation whenever you have the opportunity to do so.

• Teach your child how to do a simple examination of conscience in the evening like the one suggested on page 34. Don't forget: Always begin an examination of conscience with thanksgiving!

• If your child wants to speak to you about what he or she did wrong, be willing to listen, but if your child does not, don't ask questions. However if you have witnessed a rather important incident involving an unloving choice, you might suggest to your child that you think about his or her actions together. Simple questions might help: *What do you do think about what you did? Why did you do it? What does Jesus think about what you did? What could you have done instead to solve your problem or reach your goal? What do you want to do now?*

Always end the conversation by sharing the joy of being forgiven and reconciled so that he or she can sleep with a peace filled heart.

Supplementary activity: A celebration of forgiveness and peace

This celebration is the continuation of the thanksgiving celebration proposed in Theme 2. If possible, celebrate around the family table before the evening meal.

• Preparations

Have ready the large candle, the bouquet, and a small candle for each family member. Make sure the cards used in Theme 2 are still attached to the candles.

• The celebration

Dim the lights or close the drapes. Have the candles, the large one and the small ones, set on the table and lit.

- Introduction by a parent

Ask your child preparing for Reconciliation to recall what you did during the last celebration. If necessary, sum up what your child says and invite the family to recite together the final prayer of the Theme 2 celebration: **God our loving Parent, you share with us the joy of loving, you give us your Spirit who helps us to love a little bit as you do. We offer you our joy and give you thanks for it. Amen.**

- Penitential rite

Then continue as follows: *"Sometimes we refuse to love. We refuse to pay attention to others, to help one another, to reconcile ourselves with others. What happens on such an occasion? In our heart as well as in the entire family, there is less love and joy; it is as if God's light became dim in our home... Let us now look into our heart; let us think of a time when such a thing happened because of us. When we remember this time, we will put out our candle."*

When all have put out their candle, continue: *"For these occasions when we did not walk in God's light, when we pulled away from others and from God, let us ask forgiveness."*

- Prayer

Dear God, you know very well that at times we don't want to listen to Jesus. Days come when we break peace, when we pout, when we refuse reconciliation. Everyone is less happy then. For those days we ask forgiveness from the bottom of our heart. Amen.

Here you may sing an appropriate song such as "Lord, have mercy."

- Conclusion

As a final rite, you and your family will recall the Celebration of Reconciliation to be held soon and then relight the extinguished candles:

"Each one of us sins at some time, we break God's peace, we dim God's light in us as well as around us. That is the reason why Jesus asks us to meet together on occasion to celebrate the Sacrament of Reconciliation. In the sacrament, Jesus gives us, through the priest, a sign of God's forgiveness. We then become stronger to love, to live together in the light and joy of God. In thinking about that we will now light up our candles again and afterwards we will share a kiss of peace."

End the celebration by saying or singing the Our Father, while holding hands. Or, use the following blessing: **May the God who loves and forgives us, the God who invites us to care and to forgive others bless us and keep our heart in peace now and for ever. Amen.**

Theme Four: We Celebrate the Feast of Reconciliation
Growing in faith as adults

• Why a sacrament?

We sometimes imagine that life is where we sin, sacraments where we are forgiven. This is not so. God's free gift of love is not "fenced in" by the Liturgical Rites. It is present on all our paths. God's forgiveness is offered even before we ask, freeing and healing us as soon as we open our heart. When we love others, we love Christ, and when we reconcile with them, we return to God. The Church teaches that prayer and charity are also means of obtaining forgiveness. Why then a special Sacrament of Reconciliation if forgiveness and healing happen in daily life? Let us try to answer the question.

- An invitation to celebrate

Let us remember what we felt when we had to forgive, not a stranger, but someone dear who had hurt us deeply. How many hesitations, doubts and apprehensions we experienced! How difficult is true reconciliation! It is a kind of spiritual death. But, at last, when we "give in," what a resurrection! Joy—another name for life—is born anew between us. And we cannot know whose joy is the greater: the one who forgives or the one who is forgiven? So, why shouldn't the Church celebrate both the joy of God and the joy of the sinner? This joy is worth celebrating for this moment has great significance in our life as we are again created in love by God's own Spirit.

- A very special meeting with the Lord Jesus

Theology tells us that sacraments are acts of Christ who calls us together and gives himself to us through the sacramental signs. These actions are, therefore, priviledged meetings with Jesus. We understand that sacramental words or gestures are not magical signs. They are spiritually active and transforming because they create, deepen or re-create relationships between God, ourselves, and our neighbors.

- Words and gestures that are rooted in life and transform it

When two friends who have quarrelled decide to be reconciled, the process of reconciliation has already begun in their heart. But when they actually call up one another and meet to shake hands or speak to each other as friends again, these actions and these words accomplish, signify, and make visible to all the conversion of their heart. Thus their friendship is recreated.

We can see then the intimate link that exists between our daily life and the sacrament. The sacrament is a revelatory moment in the process of reconciliation. Rooted in our life, it expresses, celebrates, and brings to completion God's ever present forgiveness. It also expresses and celebrates our belonging to one another within the Christian

community: as we all share in the experience of sin, we are called to care for one another and to support one another.

Hopefully these brief reflections help us understand better the meaning and spiritual richness of the Sacrament of Reconciliation and renew our desire to celebrate it ourselves. This, indeed, will enable us to better share with our child the blessing and joy of the sacrament.

Understanding our children and helping them grow

• A diversity of opinions

Priests, parents, and educators have different opinions concerning the best age for celebrating Reconciliation the first time. The most recent directives coming from Rome suggest that the Bishops interpret for their own dioceses the following guidelines:

- Children should be carefully prepared, prior to their First Communion, for the Sacrament of Reconciliation.

- Children should be offered the possibility of celebrating Reconciliation.

- However, no child should be forced or even "pushed" to celebrate the sacrament.

Some people may legitimately think that children might benefit more from the Sacrament of Reconciliation by receiving it at a later age. However if children of seven to eight years of age are prepared in the right spirit and if the priest who will welcome them is also well prepared, this sacramental meeting can be a meaningful and joyful experience for the child.

• A responsibility belonging to parents

We believe that the most suitable age for celebrating this Sacrament of Reconciliation cannot be decided abstractly. All depends on each child's maturity. The Church has made a wise decision in saying that the parents, with the assistance of catechists and parish leaders, are to decide if their child is or is not ready to actually celebrate the sacrament after suitable preparation.

Some children are certainly ready at seven or eight to celebrate the sacrament. They should not be deprived of its joy. Other children are not. In fact, they might be harmed if we impose it on them. In all areas—physical, intellectual, emotional, social—children develop at their own pace. A more precocious development in any one area is not necessarily better. It is just personal; therein lies its value.

Parents should feel very free to decide what they consider is best for their child. The preparation will most certainly prove beneficial for the child even if the actual sacramental celebration is postponed for a while.

• Knowing if a child is ready for the individual celebration of the sacrament

As we said earlier, sin is a religious reality, and this is why a basic sense of right and wrong is not by itself sufficient for a child to be ready for the Sacrament of Reconciliation. When is your child ready and well prepared for personal confession?

- When your child has a genuine personal relationship with God. This means that your child is aware of being loved by God, tries to respond to that love by praying at least occasionally, is aware that God calls him or her to love and to care for others. In other words, your child must be aware that God's love and God's will have something to do with his or her everyday life and behavior.

- When your child has acquired a minimum sense of sin. For a child's misbehavior to become sin, he or she must be aware at least occasionally that when we do something wrong, we also offend God.

- When your child understands that the sacrament is a meeting with the Lord Jesus and not merely an acknowledgment of his or her faults to an authority figure like the parents or a principal.

The child coming to the sacrament must feel she or he is answering an invitation from Jesus and the community, rather than conforming to a social ritual imposed by adults.

• What happens after the first celebration?

How often should your child celebrate the sacrament after the first meeting?

- Any time your child expresses the wish, he or she should be allowed to do so. If the first experience is positive, your child may surprise you by asking to go to meet the priest more often than you thought he or she would. Then you should facilitate things for your child.

- Apart from this, when the personal initiative of the child takes the lead, encourage your child to celebrate the sacrament at special times during the Church Year like Advent or Lent, to prepare for the great feasts of Christmas and Easter. Certain special events in your child's life could also be appropriate times, like the beginning or the end of the school year, a birthday, a special feast of Our Lady or of a favorite saint.

- Finally, your child will be encouraged to join the communal celebrations offered by the parish or the school. But here again, propose, suggest, encourage but never force.

Experiencing the theme at home
• Goals

- To understand how we celebrate the Sacrament of Reconciliation.

- To be glad that we can meet the Lord in a special way in the sacrament.

• Preparations

- Do everything possible to ensure that your child has friendly contact, before the celebration, with the priest who will welcome him or her.

- Prepare what you need for a simple family celebration at home.

If the children attend a Group Session, they will be shown the Reconciliation rooms in the church so they may feel comfortable in those surroundings. If possible they will meet the priest or priests who will welcome them in individual confession. With the priest they will go through the different rites of the sacrament so they may feel more at ease when their time comes to meet with him.

• Conversations with your child

1. Read the title page, page 35. Discuss the pictures: *"Who is there? What are they doing? How do they feel? Why do they look so happy and friendly?"* Talk of the sacrament as a great gift of Jesus, a special sign of his love, an occasion for joy.

Read page 36, adding details and comments of your own to dramatize the story. Help your child to see that we can all identify with the lost sheep (*"Do we, too, sometimes take the wrong path?"*) and that Jesus is our Good Shepherd (*"Who is our Good Shepherd?"*).

Look at the pictures on page 36. Stress how happy the people seem, ask why. Point out the similarity in the two celebrations: the finding of the sheep and the feast of forgiveness.

Say together the prayer on page 37 and encourage your child to learn it by heart. Explain to your child that we can celebrate the Sacrament of Pardon in two ways: *"Whenever we want, we can find the priest on our own. We can also celebrate with our Christian community."*

2. Read pages 38 and 39. This is not the time to have your child make an examination of conscience. Instead, explain what an examination is and how we do it so as to prepare our heart for the sacrament.

3. Make sure you have enough time to read leisurely pages 40 to 44 with your child. First, go over the sequence of events in both stories: Zacchaeus' meeting with Jesus and the child's meeting with the priest. Stress each of the similarities within the events.

Come back to the first episode, look at the pictures and discuss them: *"What is each person doing and how do they feel?"* Answer any question your child has. Make sure he or she truly understands what has to be said or done at that time and why. Then, have the child complete his or her picture in the first episode. Pass on to the second episode, and so on. When you get to the third episode, the confession itself, stress that your child only needs to remember one or two sins. Reassure your child about the fear of forgetting one's sins. This is no problem. We simply ask the priest to help us remember. Stress the fact that the priest will never ever tell anyone what we told him.

Make your child familiar with the meaning of the words: confession, prayer of sorrow or contrition, absolution and penance.

Read page 44. Glance at page 45, and tell your child you will come back to it after the celebration.

Suggestions for daily life

• Maintain an atmosphere of joyful anticipation in your home, avoiding anything that might disturb your child with regard to his or her confession.

• Recite together occasionally one of the prayers proposed on page 37 or 47 of his or her book. Also recite the brief prayer of sorrow your child has chosen for the celebration.

• Make sure elder brothers or sisters don't tease your child about the coming confession but rather share in the joyous anticipation.

When the time comes for the celebration

• Before the celebration

The day before the celebration or just preceding it, if circumstances require, you might help your child prepare by using pages 38 and 39.

- Take time to pray with your child using suggestions 1 and 2 on page 38.

- Invite your child to look into his or her heart in silence while you slowly read some of the questions on page 39. Choose those that seem to you more appropriate.

- Invite your child to decide what he or she wants to tell the priest.

- Say together a prayer of sorrow as indicated on page 39. Then encourage your child to go to the priest with joy and confidence, for the Lord Jesus himself will welcome and forgive him or her.

• Just after your child's meeting with the priest

As soon as your child comes back to his or her place after meeting with the priest, welcome him or her with great affection and joy. Let your child express anything he or she wants to say.

Then invite your child to express to the Lord his or her joyful thanks.

Remind your child to do the penance the priest suggested. If it is a prayer, say it together.

• The next day

The day after the celebration, or soon afterwards have another special time with your child to start the follow-up stage.

- Read again page 44. Have your child do the drawing on page 45; help your child make a realistic decision.

- Turn back to the title page, page 35, and read it over. Then read the review on page 46. Make sure your child understands it.

- Have your child fill in page 46. Then share your impressions of the celebration and have your child do the drawing on page 47.

- You might end your conversation by reciting together the prayer on page 37 and enjoy together the last page of the book, page 48.

We must live sacraments and not only celebrate them! So, during the following weeks continue to encourage your child to keep up the good habits he or she decided upon during the preparation period, especially that of making a brief examination of conscience in the evening. Help your child be faithful. Share your child's evening prayer as often as possible.

Copyright © 1992
Novalis
6255 Hutchison
Outremont, Quebec, Canada H2V 4C7

Also distributed in Canada by:
Claude Primeau & Associates
1995 Markham Road
Scarborough, Ontario, Canada M1B 5M8

Legal Deposit:
National Library, Ottawa, Canada
National Library, Montreal, Canada

Distribution:
Novalis
49 Front Street East, 2nd Floor
Toronto, Ontario, Canada M5E 1B3

Distributed in USA by:
Franciscan Communications
1229 South Santee Street
Los Angeles, California, U.S.A. 90015

Distributed in Great Britain and Ireland by:
Geoffrey Chapman, an imprint of Cassell
Stanley House, 3 Fleets Lane
Poole, Dorset, England BH15 3A

ISBN 2-89088-568-2

Printed in Canada

This Parent Guide brochure is a part of the preparation book
for celebrating forgiveness titled *Living Reconciliation*

NOVALIS

Anita's grandparents are coming to visit this evening. This will be the first time that her grandparents will see Anita's new home.

Mother wants everything to be beautiful in the new home. She has to sew the drapes, clean up, and prepare supper. What a busy day!

Questions to think about:

- What do you think about what Anita did?

- Who did she hurt?

- What does God think about what Anita did?

- When she comes home, how will Anita feel? Why?

David is the best ball player in his class. But Luke, who is a new pupil at the school, is very good too, even though he is much smaller than David.

David begins to feel angry; he wants to be the best. He is jealous of Luke and decides to do something mean.

One evening after school David waits with a friend and they beat Luke up.

- What do you think of what David did?
- Why was beating Luke up so mean?

Sophie often misses school because of sickness. So, she has trouble when she reads outloud.

Today the teacher asks Sophie to read. She begins but soon makes mistakes.

Behind her, Lydia and Christine make fun of her...

Sophie hears them. She stops reading, turns very red, and starts to cry.

- How does Sophie feel when the others make fun of her?
- How did Lydia and Christine hurt Sophie?

Why does the Law of Love tell us not to steal, to lie, to disobey, to make fun of others or take revenge? Because when we do such things, we hurt others and also ourselves.

God loves each one of us and wants us to be happy. This is why God does not want us to do anything to hurt others and ourselves.

When We Hurt Other People, We Need to Be Forgiven.

Questions to think about:

- How does Daddy feel when he sees that the flowers are ruined?

- What does he do when Miguel comes to him?

- How does Miguel know that Daddy forgives him?
  How does this make Miguel feel?

We all do mean things sometimes, and we need to be forgiven.

Think of a time when someone you love very much forgave you. Tell about what happened in a drawing.

- How did you feel before you were forgiven? Why?

- What did you say or do to show you were sorry?

- How did you feel after being forgiven? Why?

"Let the Spirit guide you, and you will not do anything mean."

Galatians 5:16

God Always Forgives Us

"Return to me," says God,
"I will forgive you,
* I will give you a new heart."*

GO IN PEACE AND SIN NO MORE.

When we have sinned, we can turn to God with trust and ask for forgiveness. God never stops loving us; this we know for sure, thanks to Jesus.

When he lived in Galilee, Jesus was very kind to sinners and welcomed them with so much love that people were really surprised.

One day, some people brought to Jesus a woman who had been caught doing something very wrong. They wanted Jesus to punish her. But Jesus didn't. Instead, he forgave the woman and encouraged her to try to do better.

God our Father acts in the same way with us. God always loves us and always forgives us.

God Invites Us to Make Up for the Wrong We Do

God always forgives us. God says to us, "I love you; you are forgiven."

But God wants us to show the people we have hurt that we are sorry. God wants us to make up for the wrong we do.

Go back to the stories on pages 24, 25 and 26. Write or draw here how the children in those stories could make up for the harm they did.

How could Xavier make up for the wrong he did?

How could Anita make up to her mother?

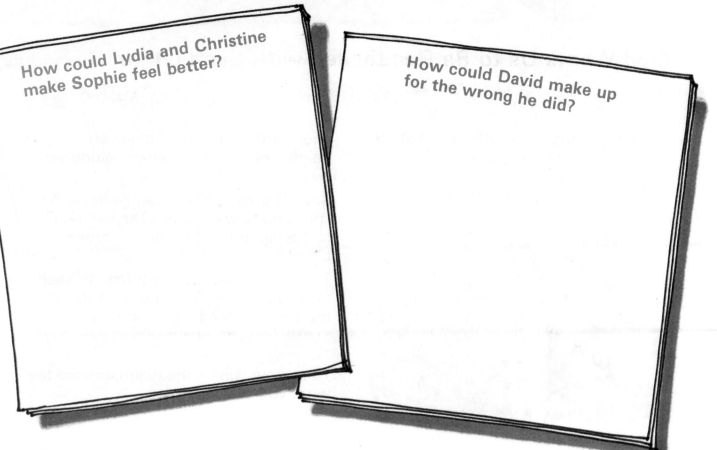

How could Lydia and Christine make Sophie feel better?

How could David make up for the wrong he did?

Remember a time when you did something really mean on purpose:

- Why did you do this mean thing?
- Whom did you hurt that day?
- When you realized what you had done, how did you feel? Why?
- How do you think Jesus felt about what you did? Why?
- What did you do to make up for the wrong you had done?
- How did you feel afterwards?

Write or draw here what you did to make up.

God Wants Us to Be Reconciled with Each Other

All of us get angry with others sometimes and turn away from them...

On Saturday morning, Vincent and Charlotte quarrelled. They even got into a fight over TV; each wanted to watch a different program.

Daddy, who was trying to get some work done, got angry, too, and sent them both to their rooms.

Questions to think about:

- What happens when we get so angry we don't want to speak to each other any more?
  Does Jesus want us to live that way?
- How do you think the Martins and the Gomez could become friends again?
- How could peace and laughter return to Vincent and Charlotte's home?

The Martins and the Gomez are neighbors. Usually they get along very well.

But, for a week now, they have not been speaking to each other. The two families had a big argument about a broken bicycle.

The parents said mean things to each other. And both families went inside their houses and were very angry.

Tomorrow will be the neighborhood fair; what will they do?

In Being Reconciled with Others, We Are Also Reconciled with God.

When we have broken friendship and joy, when we have become angry with others, God asks us to come back together and to be reconciled.
Being reconciled means to make peace, to forgive one another and to become friends again.

Remember a time when you had the courage to forgive and become reconciled. Draw about it here.

- How did you feel before you made peace? Why?
- How did you feel afterwards? Why?
- Is it hard for you to forgive others and to become reconciled with them? What do you find hard?
- Who can help you in your heart?

Have you ever noticed what we say in the "Our Father"? We say to God: "Forgive us our trespasses as we forgive those who trespass againt us."

Can we say that prayer if we really refuse to forgive and to be reconciled? What should we do before saying the prayer?

"Happy are those who make peace; truly they are God's children!"
Matthew 5:9

Completing the third step in your preparation

To follow Jesus more closely:

To review and remember:

This is what you learned:

Here are two good habits you could develop:

1. When you do something wrong on purpose and you know you hurt someone, tell Jesus right away what you did and say you are sorry.

2. Each evening, before going to sleep, talk to Jesus about your day.

- First think of all that made you happy, all the good things you did. Tell Jesus about these happy things and thank him.

- Then remember the Law of Love and ask yourself:

   "Did I do something on purpose that hurt someone?

   Did I refuse to listen to the Spirit of Jesus today?"

   If you did anything wrong, tell Jesus about it. Then tell him you are sorry and ask for his help to do better tomorrow.

   If you pray like this, day after day, Jesus will help you grow in love. You will be happy and make people around you happy too.

- When we refuse to listen to the Spirit of Jesus, when we do something wrong on purpose, we commit a sin.

- God does not want us to sin because sin hurts us and others, too.

- God is always ready to forgive us, God never stops loving us.

- God wants us to make up for the harm we do to others and to forgive those who hurt us.

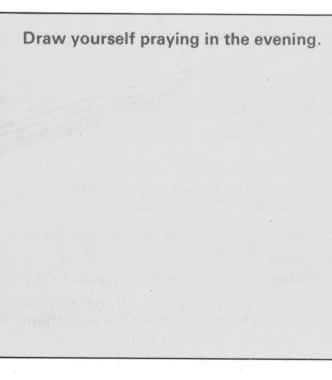

Draw yourself praying in the evening.

To help you pray:

O Loving God, I am sorry for the wrong things I have done and for the good things I have not done. Please forgive me. Open my heart to your Spirit and help me grow in love. I ask you this through your Son Jesus. Amen.

4 We Celebrate the Sacrament of Reconciliation

A smile, a friendly word, a warm welcome, a beautiful surprise,
all of these can be signs of forgiveness.

What joy in our heart when we receive such a sign,
when we are sure we are forgiven!

The Lord Jesus, who knows us well, wanted to leave us
with a special sign of God's forgiveness.
This sign is ours in the Sacrament of Reconciliation.

How wonderful to share a beautiful celebration of Forgiveness!
How great to walk together again in joy and friendship!

Come, Let Us Rejoice!

1. Once a shepherd had 100 sheep. He loved them very much and took good care of them.

   One evening, as usual, he counted his sheep: *"...97, 98, 99!"*

   "But where is my hundredth sheep? Clearly, it is lost". Right away, the shepherd set out to look for his little lost sheep.

2. At long last, the shepherd found his sheep. He was very, very happy. He took the sheep in his arms, spoke to it gently and carried it home on his shoulders.

3. Passing through the village, he called out to his friends and invited them to rejoice with him.

   "Thus,"* says Jesus, *"there is great rejoicing in heaven when each one of you comes back to the Lord and asks for forgiveness." Based on Matthew 18:12-14

- What did the shepherd do for his lost sheep?

- Why did he rejoice with his friends?

- What does Jesus, our Good Shepherd, do for us when we forget about the Law of Love?

Let Us Celebrate God's Forgiveness!

Here are some Christians celebrating together the Sacrament of Reconciliation. They tell God they are sorry for their sins. They sing their joy at being forgiven. They also ask the Holy Spirit to help them follow the Law of Love.

In the name of Jesus, our Good Shepherd, the priest welcomes them warmly.
He invites them to change the way they live. He gives them a special sign of God's forgiveness.

When you want to, you can join with your Christian community, or go to the priest on your own, to celebrate the great love of God who always forgives us.

Prayer

**Lord Jesus,
you are my Good Shepherd.
You are always with me,
I will not be afraid.
You guide me on paths of joy.
I shall be happy with you
for ever and ever. Amen.**

Here Is How to Prepare Yourself for the Sacrament of Reconciliation

When we want a celebration to be wonderful, we have to prepare carefully. We do this, too, with the Sacrament of Forgiveness.

Everything you have done for the last few weeks, both at home and in class, has helped you to understand better God's great love and God's call. And so now the time has come for you to prepare your heart for a very special encounter with the Lord Jesus in the Sacrament of Reconciliation.

Choose a quiet time to do it the day before the celebration or before going to church. You will find on these two pages step by step directions which will make your preparation easy and enjoyable.

Find a quiet place time so you will not be disturbed. Let the peace of God fill your heart and rejoice,

THE LORD IS WITH YOU!

1. Remember Jesus' call

Jesus invites you to follow him, he gives you his Spirit so you can love God and other people just like he did.

When you answer Jesus' call, your heart is filled with joy. Give thanks to God for that joy.

2. Pray to the Holy Spirit

Holy Spirit, please help me to understand Jesus' call, to know my sins and be sorry for them with all my heart. Amen.

3. Remember your sins

Think about Jesus, think about the Law of Love. Then ask yourself:

- Do I forget to pray to God each day?
- Do I refuse to be reconciled after becoming angry?
- Do I disobey on purpose?
- Do I sometimes hurt others

  by stealing, by lying,

  by making fun of them,

  by fighting, especially with those younger than me,

  by leading them to do wrong,

  by spoiling the world in which we live?

- Do I sometimes close my heart to others

  by refusing to help them,

  by refusing to share with them,

  by refusing to forgive them?

  Remember: We only sin when we do something wrong on purpose.

4. Ask for God's forgiveness

In your own words, tell God you are sorry for your sins. Or, if you wish, you might say the following prayer:

**Dear God,
I am sorry for doing wrong.
Please forgive me all my sins.
I know you love me very much.
Help me love you in return
and care for others as you do. Amen.**

Now your heart is ready, you can go with joy to meet the Lord Jesus in the Sacrament of Reconciliation.

Anytime you wish to celebrate this Sacrament again, you might like to use these two pages 38 and 39 to help you prepare.

What You Will Do in the Sacrament of Reconciliation

Recalling the beautiful story of Zacchaeus will help you understand what happens in the Sacrament of Reconciliation.

Zacchaeus Meets with Jesus:

1. Zacchaeus is eager to know Jesus. Jesus is happy to go to Zacchaeus' house. Jesus wants him to become a friend.

2. Zacchaeus listens to Jesus speak of God's mercy and of the Law of Love.

3. Zacchaeus understands that he is a sinner. He speaks to Jesus with great trust for Zacchaeus knows that Jesus loves him.

You Meet with the Priest:

1. The priest welcomes you.

You return his greetings. You might make the Sign of the Cross together.

Finish the pictures so the child looks like you.

2. You share the Word of God.

God's Word helps us to learn about God's love and about the Law of Love.

3. You confess your sins.

Speak with trust. You are opening your heart to Jesus himself. What you tell the priest will remain a secret between you and him.

If you have forgotten your sins, don't worry; the priest will help you remember them.

Zacchaeus Meets with Jesus:

4. Zacchaeus promises Jesus that he will make up for his sins and change his ways.

5. The Lord Jesus forgives Zacchaeus all his sins.

   Zacchaeus is so happy to be forgiven and to know Jesus better!
   He wants to be Jesus' friend forever.

6. At the end of the meal, Zacchaeus thanks Jesus with great joy.

   Jesus, too, is happy to have made a new friend.

You Meet with the Priest:

4. The priest encourages you to try to do better.

He helps you to see what you can do to make up for your sins. You agree to do something special. This is your penance.

5. The priest gives you the sign of God's forgiveness.

First you say a prayer of sorrow.

Then you listen carefully as the priest says the words of absolution. These words are the sign that God forgives you.

During the absolution you might make the Sign of the Cross. At the end, you answer "Amen."

6. With the priest you give thanks to God.

You say a prayer of praise. The priest wishes you peace. You thank him and leave.

Finish the pictures, as you did on page 41.

After the Celebration of Reconciliation

God has forgiven you. The Spirit of Jesus has given you
new strength to live by the Law of Love, to build a better world,
a world of friendship and joy, a world like God wants it to be.

To prepare for the great feast of Easter,
Florence and Richard celebrate
the Sacrament of Reconciliation.

They think about how they have hurt
others. They speak with the priest. Now
they know better how they will listen to
the Spirit of Jesus.

Florence decides she will play more often
with her little sister on the weekends.
Then her mother can relax and do things
she enjoys.

Richard is going to stop making fun of
Roger, who can't play ball very well.
Instead, Richard will show Roger how to
play better.

What About You

Now you too have celebrated
the Sacrament of Reconciliation.
What will you do to try to love
both God and other people better?

Think about this and draw
two things you might do.

To review and remember

- In the Sacrament of Reconciliation
  the Lord Jesus gives us, through the priest,
  a special sign of God's forgiveness.

- Any time we want to, we can go to the priest
  to receive the sign of God's forgiveness.

- Sometimes our parish community invites us
  to celebrate together the Sacrament of Reconciliation.

- The Church encourages us to prepare
  for the great feasts of the year
  by celebrating Reconciliation.

- When we celebrate the Sacrament of Pardon,
  God gives us special help so that we can
  share peace and love with others.

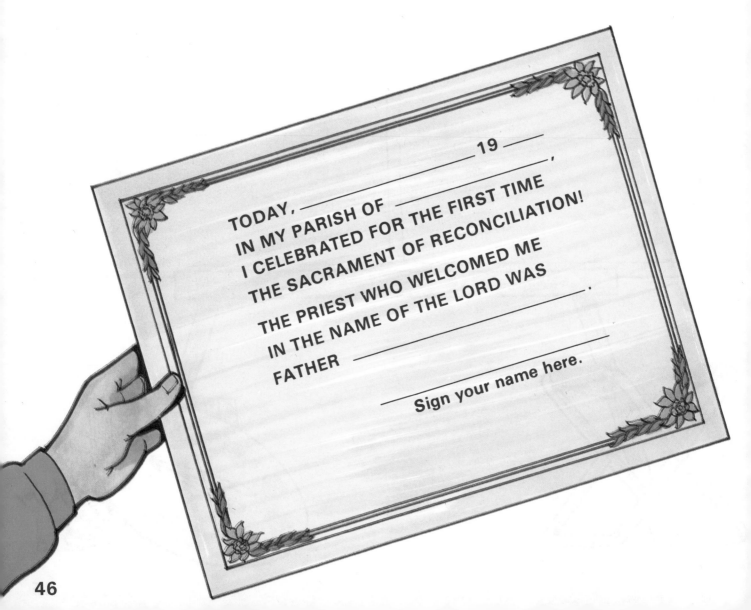

TODAY, _____ 19 ___ ,
IN MY PARISH OF _____,
I CELEBRATED FOR THE FIRST TIME
THE SACRAMENT OF RECONCILIATION!

THE PRIEST WHO WELCOMED ME
IN THE NAME OF THE LORD WAS

FATHER _____.

_____
Sign your name here.

Write or draw what you liked most about the Celebration of Reconciliation:

"O God, you do wonderful things for me; I give you thanks and praise!" Based on Psalms 66

Sing and dance for the Lord, all people of the earth!
God loves us, God forgives us,
God's own joy is in our heart!